HENRY AND THE HELICOPTER

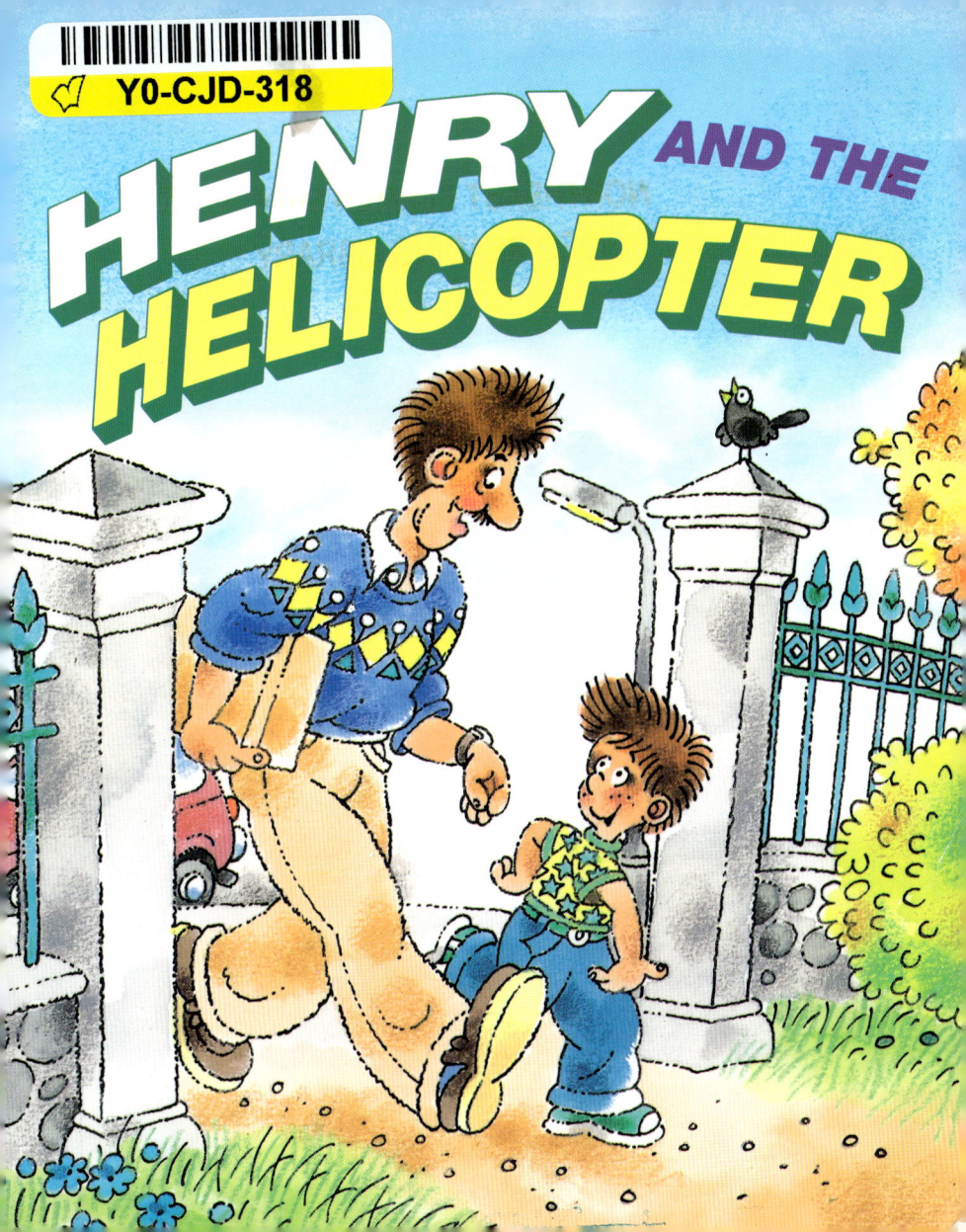

Henry watched the helicopter.

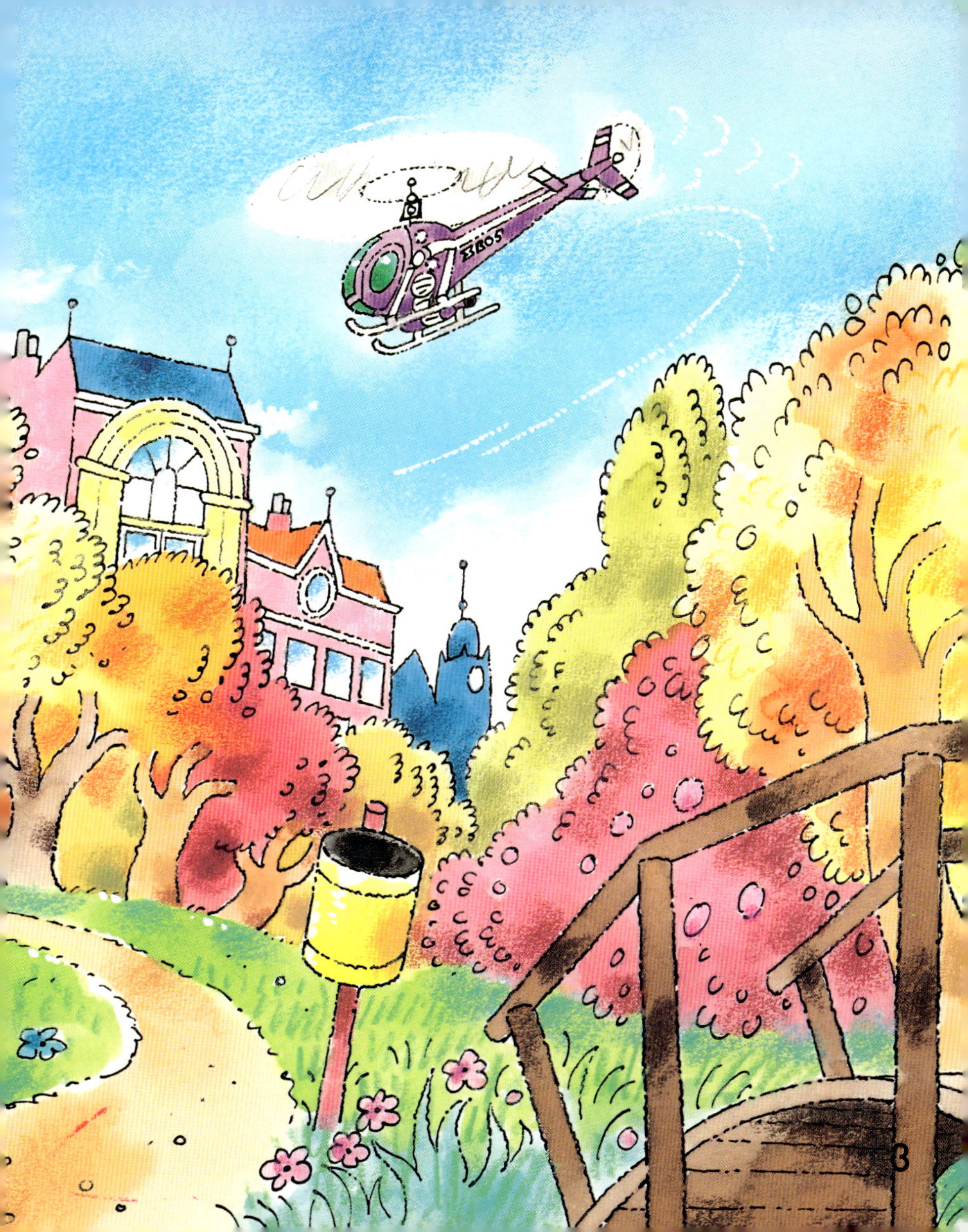

He watched the helicopter fly above the buildings.

5

He watched the helicopter fly above the trees.

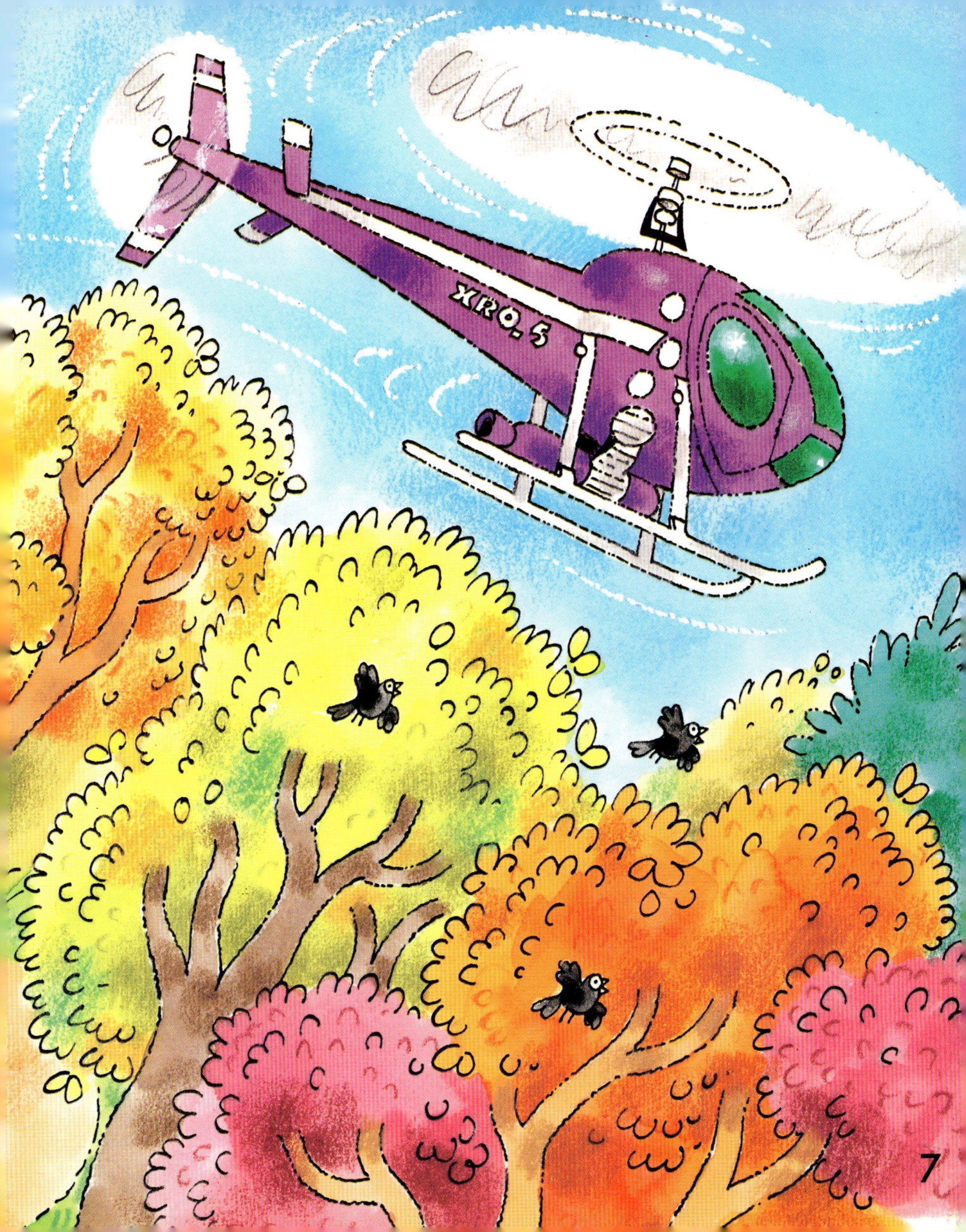
XRO. 5

He watched the helicopter fly above the park.

9

Then something went wrong.

11

The helicopter crashed into the park bench.

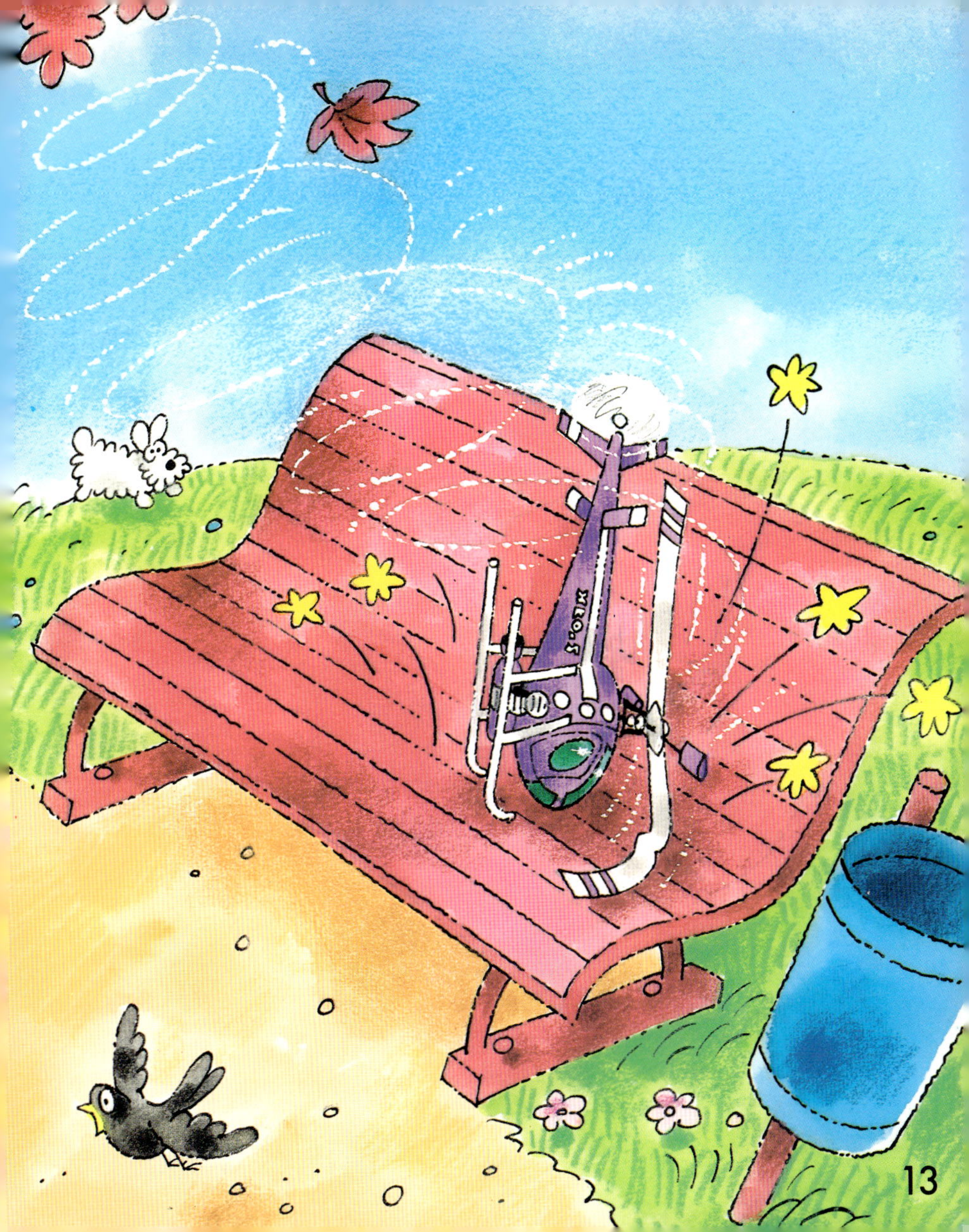

"Oh no," said Henry.

"I can fix it,"
said Henry's father.

"Can I fly it this time?"
said Henry.